There are around 500 species of oak tree. You can tell them apart by their leaves, acorns, and bark.

So, how are trees like people?
   Great question! Well, let's take a look over here

Oak trees are home to 100's of animals. *That's right, insects are animals!*

One of the smallest is the acorn weevil. It burrows into an acorn and lays its eggs so when they hatch they can feed on the seed inside.

The acorn weevil's larva is one of nature's most beautiful creations.... No it's not! I just made that up! It's a squirmy looking thing, like all larvae.

A patch of milkweed grows next to a root. Milkweed leaves are the only food that a monarch caterpillar will eat—without milkweed it cannot turn into a butterfly.

Monarchs travel 2500 miles from the U.S. to Mexico to hibernate during the winter months. Most fly, while others go by train or bus.

Butterflies smell and taste with their feet. You could say they have smelly feet!

An oak tree can be home to 1000's of caterpillars, all of which turn into either a moth or a butterfly.

One of these creepy crawlers is the striped hairstreak.

I'm a grown-up hairstreak caterpillar!

This butterfly has evolved an eyespot and false antennae so that birds mistake the back for the front.

A troop of carpenter ants marches toward a decaying limb. They will build their home here (mostly condos). Unlike termites they do not eat the wood they burrow into, but rather build their nests in the hollowed out spaces.

Honey bees return home after a day collecting nectar (for energy) and pollen (for protein and other nutrients). They are attracted to yellow, blue, and purple flowers.

There are over 20,000 species of bees, 8 of which are honey bees. 90% of bees are solitary.

All bees are important pollinators for many fruits, vegetables, and nuts (as are birds, bats, and butterflies. Together they tour as "The 4B Pollinators").

Many kinds of birds call the oak tree home. The acorn woodpecker is one of them. They live in groups and depend mainly on acorns for food. They store the acorns in small holes drilled into trees, telephone poles, or wooden buildings.

Red bellied woodpeckers build their nests in tree hollows. Once finished it's time for a late night snack.

Screech owls will roost in natural cavities in large trees. Despite their size (6-10 inches) they are quite fearsome. Early explorers nicknamed them the "feathered wildcats."

Blue jays are noisy and aggressive. They are also curious and intelligent. They can crack open an acorn with their strong black beaks.

Squirrels bury a lot of acorns to be eaten in the future, especially in the winter months. They lose track of many of these buried nuts which can then sprout into a tree.

Opossum families can be found nesting in the branches. They can hang by their tails, but only briefly. They do not sleep upside down.

Bats will often snooze during the day while hanging by their toes. Bats, sloths, and manatees are the only mammals that sleep upside down.

Raccoons find tree hollows a cozy way to spend the winter. They frequently order take-out during the cold winter months, Rocky's being a favorite.

Foxes also seek shelter in the hollows of a tree. This family has made a home beneath a large root and are seen here preparing to watch their favorite TV show.

Deer, black bears, badgers, wood ducks, wild turkeys, and many others all enjoy an acorn meal.

A BONUS page with lots of words!

This is the Pechanga Great Oak, a coastal live oak found in Temecula, Ca. It is sacred to the Pechanga Band of the Luiseña Indian tribe.

It is 100 ft. tall and may be the world's oldest living oak. The term "live oak" comes from the fact that it replaces its leaves throughout the year—it is never leafless.

On the front cover is the Major Oak, an English oak found in Sherwood Forest. Legend has it that Robin Hood used it as a hiding place.

The Major is 900 years old.

Angel Oak is on the title page. Local folklore tells of ghosts of former slaves appearing as angels around the tree.

The Angel is 400-500 yrs. old and is considered one of the world's most beautiful oak trees. You can find it on Johns Island, S. Carolina.

On the back cover is the Seven Sisters Oak, named after the seven Doby sisters—owners of the property. There are seven large trunks—one for each sister—flowing outward from a common base.

The Seven Sisters resides in Mandeville, La. It is around 800 yrs. old and has a 40 ft. circumference.

To Our Blue Planet's Green Canopy

The Oaks
Copyright ©2025 Dr. Rob Cardwell
ISBN-13: 978-1-7377407-6-6

All rights reserved. This book may not be reproduced in whole or in part in any form, or by any means, without express written permission from the publisher.

Published by Dr. Rob Cardwell
P.O. Box 1855
Ocean City, NJ 08226

You can visit our picture book family at:
docspicturebooks.com

www.ingramcontent.com/pod-product-compliance
Lightning Source LLC
Chambersburg PA
CBRC102224090526
44583CB00010BA/192